LET'S GO FISHING

IN STREAMS, RIVERS, AND LAKES

GEORGE TRAVIS

The Rourke Corporation, Inc.
Vero Beach, Florida 32964

CS CD TH CM DA JS

PHOTO CREDITS
© Wisconsin Department of Tourism: page 19; © Duane C. Hoven/ Wisconsin Department of Tourism: page 15; © Hal Kern/International Stock: cover; © Mark Bolster/International Stock: page 10; © Dusty Willison/International Stock: page 12; © Greg Voight/International Stock: page 16; © East Coast Studios: pages 4, 6, 7, 9, 13, 18

FISH ILLUSTRATIONS: © Duane Raver

PROJECT EDITOR: Duane Raver
Duane Raver received a degree in Zoology with a major in fishery management from Iowa State University. Employed by the North Carolina Wildlife Resources Commission as a fishery biologist in 1950, he transferred to the Education Division in 1960. He wrote and illustrated for the magazine *Wildlife in North Carolina*. Mr. Raver retired as the editor in 1979 and is a freelance writer and illustrator.

EDITORIAL SERVICES: Penworthy Learning Systems

Library of Congress Cataloging-in-Publication Data

Travis, George. 1961-
 Let's go fishing in streams, rivers, and lakes / by George Travis.
  p. cm. — (Let's go fishing)
 Includes index
 Summary: Describes the equipment and techniques used in freshwater fishing.
  ISBN 0-86593-465-7
  1. Fishing—Juvenile literature. 2. Rivers—Juvenile literature.
3. Lakes—Juvenile literature. [1. Fishing.] I. Title.
II. Series: Travis, George, 1961- Let's go fishing.
SH445.T735 1998
799.1'1—dc21   97–51918
                                                   CIP
                                                   AC

Printed in the USA

14.75

TABLE OF CONTENTS

FISHING IN FRESH WATER

One of the best things about freshwater fishing is almost anyone can do it! The basic skills are easy to learn. If you don't have a boat, you can fish from the shore or by carefully wading in shallow water.

There are several kinds of freshwater fishing—fly fishing, **lure** (LOOR) fishing, often called "bait-casting," pole fishing, and fishing with a hook and line. Which one you choose depends on the area you are fishing in and the kinds of fish you are hoping to catch.

You don't need a boat to fish in this pond!

RODS & REELS

The equipment used in fishing is called tackle. *Basic* tackle is a rod, reel, line, hook, or lure.

Most rods, or poles, are made from very light man-made materials. Some rods are one piece, while others have two or more pieces, making them easier to carry when you are not fishing.

Docks make a great place to fish, but be careful.

Reels wind in the line when you have hooked a fish.

The **reel** (REEL) is attached to the rod. The fishing line winds around the **spool** (SPOOL) of the reel. The spool lets you release your line carefully and quickly when casting, and wind in the line when bringing in a fish.

Some reels, like fly fishing reels, are simple. They have no gears, just a handle to wind in the line. Other reels may have a lot of gears and a spool with an electric motor.

IN YOUR TACKLE BOX

Tackle boxes come in many different sizes. They are made of metal, wood, or plastic. A tackle box has many **compartments** (kum PAHRT munts) to hold small fishing items like hooks, lures, and floats. Your things will stay organized and safe in the box.

A tackle box is also a good place to keep clippers or pliers, for cutting line and fixing tackle. You might take a knife, too, for cutting bait or cleaning fish.

You can take along a small scale and a tape measure for measuring the fish you catch, too.

A tackle box will keep your things safe and organized.

WORMS & THINGS

Bait is attached to a hook at the end of the line. Bait fools the fish into biting on the hook and getting caught. If you want to catch fish, you have to use the right bait.

Most **artificial** (AHR tuh FISH ul) bait—lures and flies—looks like the fish's natural food. Artificial bait comes in many different styles and colors and has one or more hooks.

Some people like to use **natural** (NACH ur ul) bait. Natural bait can be anything from small baitfish and shrimp to insects and worms. You can buy natural bait from most tackle stores or gather it yourself for free. Bread or canned meat may also be good bait for certain kinds of fish.

Learning to choose the right lures takes practice.

READING THE WATER

Experienced **anglers** (ANG glerz) know how to "read" the water. They know the signs of where fish are.

Fish will go where they can feed safely. In lakes, for example, weed beds, reeds, and water lilies are favorite places for fish to feed.

You have a good chance of catching fish around lilies, logs, and grasses.

This angler has found a calm spot for fishing in this river.

Trees and logs that have fallen in the water are good places, too.

In rivers, fish like to live where the water doesn't flow too fast. They also like water that is deep enough that they can hide from their **predators** (PRED uh turz), like birds and mammals.

Fish do not like brightly lit water. They have no eyelids so they cannot close out the bright light.

CASTING YOUR LINE

Casting is the skill of throwing the bait and line through the air. You try to place your bait exactly where you want it in the water.

There are different ways of casting. If you know any experienced anglers, ask them to show you how to cast. Skill is more important than strength, and it will take practice.

Remember to watch for trees, bushes, *and* people behind you when you cast. The only thing you want to hook is a fish! Also pay attention to where other anglers are fishing. So you don't get your line tangled with theirs.

The low light of dusk is a perfect time to catch fish.

IS IT A KEEPER?

A float, or bobber, on your line will tell you when a fish has your bait. The tug of the fish will make the float bob up and down. Just as in casting, reeling in a fish takes practice and skill. Lots of fish get away.

Sometimes fish get away because the knot holding the hook to the line comes undone. Learn how to tie knots and practice them.

Many places have catch-and-release laws that protect fish from **extinction** (ex TINGK shun). These laws mean that if you catch a fish, you must return it to the water without harming it. People often take a picture of their fish and write down its weight and length. This way they have a record of the biggest fish they have caught.

This fish is about to be let go—and may be caught again someday.

KNOW THE RULES

Every state has free copies of its fishing laws. The laws are different in each state. You should read them *before* you go fishing. The laws will tell you if you need a fishing license; if there is a fishing season; and what fish, if any, you may keep.

Stay on top of the rules—they are always changing.

For safety, children must wear life jackets when riding in a boat.

Other important things to remember: do not leave your trash behind, and *never* leave old fishing line. The line could wrap around birds or small animals, and may injure them. Hooks are very dangerous to leave behind, too. Animals can step on or swallow them.

Before you fish on private property, always get permission from the landowner.

SAFETY

Anytime you are around deep or fast-moving water, you should wear a life jacket. If you are on a boat, follow boating rules. Be aware of changing weather, too. Don't get caught in a bad storm.

Sunblock and insect repellent are good items to keep in your tackle box, along with a first-aid kit.

Be careful when handling fish, like catfish, that have sharp **spines** (SPYNZ). You don't want a spine to stick your foot or hand. Some fish have sharp teeth. Watch out for them!

Follow the simple rules, and use common sense. You'll soon discover how much fun fishing can be.

fish: black crappie *(Pomoxis nigromaculatus)*
average weight: 12 oz. to 1 lb., 8 oz.
(340 to 680 grams)
location: eastern North
America from southern
Canada to the Gulf

---

fish: channel catfish *(Ictalurus punctatus)*
average weight: 3 to 5 lbs.
(1.4 to 2.3 kilograms), may
reach 60 lbs. (27 kilograms)
location: Great Lakes to
and Gulf Slope drainages

---

fish: common (or king) carp *(Cyprinus carpio)*
average weight: 5 to 10 lbs.
(2.3 to 4.5 kilograms), may reach
80 lbs. (36 kilograms)
location: Most of Eurasia;
North America, South Africa, India,
Australia and New Zealand

---

fish: muskellunge *(Esox masquinongy)*
average weight: 15 to 25 lbs.
(6.8 to 11.3 kilograms), may
reach 70 lbs. (31.8 kilograms)
location: Great Lakes region, Mississippi basin, Atlantic
drainages south to Georgia and Virginia

fish: pumkinseed *(Lepomis gibbosus)*
average weight: may reach
1 lb., 1 oz. (482 grams)
location: the Dakotas and Iowa
to the Atlantic drainages

---

fish: rainbow trout *(Oncorhynchus mykiss)*
average weight: 2 to 8 lbs.
(.9 to 3.6 kilograms)
location: mostly from
Alaska to California,
northeast Asia; elsewhere in
North America, Europe, South America, Australia, New
Zealand, Africa, and India

---

fish: smallmouth bass *(Micropterus dolomieui)*
average weight: 2 to 3 lbs. (.9 to 1.4 kilograms), may reach
12 lbs. (5.4 kilograms)
location: from North Dakota
to Québec, south to
Oklahoma, and Alabama

---

fish: white bass *(Morone chrysops)*
average weight: 8 oz. to 2 lbs.
(227 to 907 grams)
location: Manitoba and
Québec to the Gulf

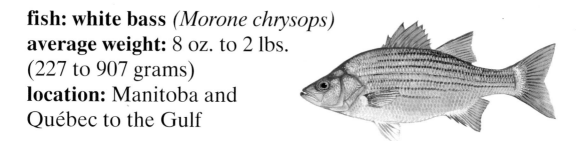

GLOSSARY

anglers (ANG glerz) — people who fish

artificial (AHR tuh FISH ul) — made by human beings rather than nature

compartment (kum PAHRT munt) — a section or part of an area set apart by walls

extinction (ex TINGK shun) — no longer existing; the complete disappearance of a living plant or animal

lure (LOOR) — man-made bait used to attract and catch fish

natural (NACH ur ul) — produced by or found in nature

predators (PRED uh turz) — animals that eat other animals

reel (REEL) — a spool-like device that winds up fishing line

spines (SPYNZ) — part of a plant or animal that sticks out with a sharp point

spool (SPOOL) — the part of a reel that holds fishing line

INDEX

FURTHER READING:

Find out more about fishing with these helpful books and information sites:
The Dorling Kindersley Encyclopedia of Fishing. The Complete Guide to the Fish, Tackle, & Techniquies of Fresh & Saltwater Angling. Dorling Kindersley, Inc., 1994
Griffen, Steven A., *The Fishing Sourcebook: Your One-Stop Resource for Everything You Need to Feed Your Fishing Habit.* The Globe Pequot Press, 1996
Price, Steven D. *The Ultimate Fishing Guide.* HarperCollins, 1996
Waszczuk, Henry and Labignan, Halto. *Freshwater Fishing. 1000 Tips from the Pros.* Key Porter Books, 1993
National Marine Fisheries Service online at www.nmfs.gov
World of Fishing online at www.fishingworld.com